Learning about Cats

THE PERSIAN CAT

by Joanne Mattern

Consultant:
Wanda Roe
Persian and Himalayan Cat Rescue
Mill Valley, California

CAPSTONE BOOKS
an imprint of Capstone Press
Mankato, Minnesota

Capstone Books are published by Capstone Press
151 Good Counsel Drive, P.O. Box 669, Mankato, Minnesota 56002
http://www.capstone-press.com

Library of Congress Cataloging-in-Publication Data

Mattern, Joanne, 1963–
    The Persian cat/by Joanne Mattern.
    p.cm.—(Learning about cats)
    Includes bibliographical references (p. 45) and index.
    Summary: Discusses the history, development, habits, and care of Persian cats.
    ISBN 0-7368-0566-4
    1. Persian cat—Juvenile literature. [1. Persian cat. 2. Cats. 3. Pets] I. Title.
II. Series.

SF449.P4 M38 2001
636.8'32—dc21   00-022979

Editorial Credits
Angela Kaelberer, editor; Linda Clavel, cover designer and illustrator; Katy Kudela,
    photo researcher

Photo Credits
International Stock/Tetsu Yamakazi, cover, 22, 28
Norvia Behling, 4, 6, 10, 24, 31, 38
Ron Kimball/Ron Kimball Studios, 9, 12, 14, 16, 19, 20, 27, 33, 37, 40–41
Root Resources/Laurie Myhre-Choate, 34

Table of Contents

Quick Facts about the Persian

Description

Size: Persian cats have short, muscular bodies. They are medium-sized cats.

Weight: Adult Persians weigh 5 to 15 pounds (2.3 to 6.8 kilograms).

Physical features: The Persian has a coat of long, silky fur. It has a ruff of longer fur around its neck. The Persian's legs are short and strong. Its head is large and round. The Persian's nose is short and can give its face a flat, pushed-in appearance.

Color:	Persians can be one or more of a number of colors. Common Persian colors include black, chocolate or brown, blue, red, cream, silver, gold, and white. Persians also can have different markings. Some Persians have light-colored coats with darker faces, ears, paws, and tails. These Persians are called Himalayans.

Development

Place of origin:	Many people believe that the Persian breed came from Persia. This region of Asia now is the country of Iran.
History of breed:	Persians and other longhaired cats first lived in Asian regions such as Persia and Turkey. In the 1500s, sailors and merchants brought these cats to Europe. Persians quickly became popular in Europe. People brought Persians to North America during the late 1800s.
Numbers:	In 1999, the Cat Fanciers' Association (CFA) registered 30,656 Persians worldwide. This number includes Himalayans. Owners who register their Persians record the cats' breeding records with an official club. The CFA is the world's largest organization of cat breeders.

Chapter 1

The Persian Cat

The Persian has been the most popular cat breed in North America for many years. Many people appreciate this breed's beauty and quiet, calm personality.

Appearance

Persians are medium-sized cats. Their bodies are stocky and low to the ground. Their legs are short and sturdy. They have large, round paws.

A Persian's coat is one of its most attractive features. The cat has a double coat. Its fur is thick and plush near the skin. This thick layer of fur is covered by lighter, silky fur. Persians require daily grooming to keep their coats healthy and attractive.

The Persian has a double coat of fur.

A Persian's coat is heavier during the winter. During spring and summer, Persians shed this heavier coat for a cooler, lighter coat.

The Persian's large, round face is another distinctive feature. Some people think the Persian's large eyes and short nose give its face a sweet expression.

Personality

Persians are known for their calm personalities. The Persian is among the quietest and least active of all cat breeds. Persians also are gentle and good-natured. They rarely fight with people or other animals.

Persians are friendly, affectionate cats. They seem to enjoy sitting on people's laps or being petted.

Persians can live in a variety of households. Their quiet personality makes them best suited for calm, quiet households. But they can adapt to living in households with children. Persians also get along well with dogs and other cats.

Some people believe the Persian's features give it a sweet expression.

Chapter 2

Development of the Breed

The Persian probably descended from longhaired Asian cats. Manuscripts and drawings from as early as 1684 B.C. show cats that look like Persians. Some interesting legends or stories about where this breed came from also exist.

A Magical Legend

One legend tells the story of a merchant who came across a group of robbers attacking a stranger. The merchant fought off the thieves and cared for the injured stranger. After he recovered, the stranger told the merchant that he was a magician. He promised the merchant one wish in payment for saving his life. But the merchant did not want a wish. He was happy with his life. He told the magician that he liked to sit under the

The Persian may have descended from longhaired Asian cats.

Today, the Persian is the most popular breed in the world.

sparkling stars at night. He liked to watch the smoke swirl from a crackling fire.

The magician said that he could give the merchant a gift of just those things. He took a swirl of smoke, a spear of fire, and the light of two stars. The magician then created a cat with a fire-tipped tongue, smoke-gray fur, and sparkling eyes. It was the first Persian cat.

The Real Story

In the 1500s, European sailors and merchants often traveled to the Asian regions of Turkey and Persia. Persia now is the country of Iran. These sailors and merchants brought longhaired cats back to Europe. The Turkish cats were called Angoras. The cats from Persia were called Persians. Both of these longhaired cats soon became popular with European royal families.

Early Angoras and Persians looked much alike. But differences between the two breeds developed by the late 1800s. Persians were heavier than Angoras. Their coats were thicker. Persians also had larger heads and rounder eyes than Angoras.

The Breed Develops

By 1903, Persians were recognized as a separate breed in Great Britain. But they were called longhairs instead of Persians. Today, British people still call Persian cats longhairs.

After 1895, people brought Persians to North America from Europe. The Persian soon became North America's most popular breed. More Persians are registered with the Cat Fanciers' Association than any other breed.

Chapter 3

Today's Persian

Today, Persians are the best known and most popular cat breed in the world. These cats often are exhibited in cat shows. But not every Persian can compete in these shows.

Changes in Appearance

The Persian breed has changed during the past 100 years. Today's Persians have a shorter, more compact body than the Persians of the early 1900s. Their fur also has changed. Today's Persians have much thicker, longer fur than the original Persians. A Persian's outer coat can be 6 to 8 inches (15 to 20 centimeters) long.

The biggest change in the Persian's appearance is in its face. Early Persians had wedge-shaped heads with long noses. But

Today's Persians have much thicker, longer fur than the original Persians did.

The Persian's short nose makes the cat's face look almost flat.

today's Persians have larger, more rounded heads. Their noses are much shorter. Persians' short noses makes their faces look almost flat.

Breeding and Heredity
These changes in the Persian's appearance occurred because of careful work by cat breeders. Breeders choose cats with specific traits that they want to continue in the breed.

These physical features can include color, coat length, or eye shape. Breeders then mate male and female cats that have these traits. The breeders hope that the resulting kittens will have the preferred traits. The entire appearance of a breed can change over the years through selective breeding.

Persians also have been used to create new breeds. For example, the Exotic breed began by breeding Persians with American Shorthairs. The Exotic breed looks like a shorthaired Persian. Mating other breeds with Persians can introduce new colors into the other breed. This process also can change the breed's body shape or fur length.

Breed Standard

Judges look for certain physical features when they judge Persians in cat shows. These features are called the breed standard.

The breed standard says that the Persian should have a broad, muscular body. Its legs must be short and sturdy. Its head should be large and round. A Persian should have large, round eyes and small, rounded ears. Its nose must be short and broad. Its tail should be short. The fur on the tail should be thick.

A Persian's coat should be long, thick, and glossy. The coat's texture must be fine. The ruff of fur around the neck should come to a point between the front legs.

Color Divisions

The Cat Fanciers' Association divides Persians into seven color divisions for competition. These divisions are solid, shaded and smoke, tabby, bi-color, parti-color, silver and golden, and Himalayan.

Solid-color Persians have undercoats and overcoats of one solid color. These colors may be white, black, blue, red, cream, chocolate, or lilac. Blue Persians have gray coats. Chocolate Persians have brown coats. Lilac Persians have pink-gray coats.

Shaded Persians have white coats with colored tips at the end of each hair. These tips can be red, cream, black, or blue. Some shaded Persians have two or more colors of tips.

Smoke Persians often appear to be one color. But they actually have a white undercoat with a

Tabby Persians have coats with darker striped markings.

darker solid overcoat. This overcoat can be black, blue, cream, red, blue-cream, or tortoiseshell. Tortoiseshell Persians' overcoats have patches of black, red, and cream fur.

Tabby Persians have coats with darker striped markings. Their coats can be silver, red, brown, blue, cream, or blue-cream.

Bi-color Persians have coats with patches of white and another solid color. These colors

The Himalayan resulted from mating Persian and Siamese cats.

include black, blue, cream, red, chocolate, or lilac.

Parti-color Persians' coats have patches of two or more colors. These color combinations include tortoiseshell, blue-cream, chocolate tortoiseshell, and lilac-cream.

Special Types of Persians

Some types of Persians differ from other Persians in ways other than color. These types are silver and golden Persians and Himalayans.

Silver Persians have white coats. But each hair has a black tip. This coloring makes the cat's coat appear silver. Golden Persians have cream coats with black tips.

Silver and golden Persians have features not found in other Persians. Silver and golden Persians' faces are less flat than those of other Persians. Silver and golden Persians also have thick black rims around their eyes.

The Himalayan resulted from mating Persian and Siamese cats. Himalayans have the Persian's compact body, long fur, and flat face. Both Siamese and Himalayans have light-colored coats with dark fur on their ears, face, paws, and tail. These darker areas are called colorpoints. All Siamese and Himalayan cats have blue eyes.

The Cat Fanciers' Association considers Himalayans to be part of the Persian breed. But some other cat organizations consider Himalayans to be a separate breed. These groups include the Canadian Cat Association and The International Cat Association.

Chapter 4

Owning a Persian

People can adopt Persians in several ways. They may contact breeders, pet stores, animal shelters, or rescue organizations. Persians from breeders or pet stores can cost several hundred dollars. Animal shelters or breed rescue organizations can be less expensive places to adopt Persians.

Persian Breeders

People who want a show-quality Persian should buy one from a breeder. Most breeders carefully select their cats for breeding. People who buy a kitten from a breeder often can meet the kitten's parents. This gives owners an idea of how the kitten will look and behave as an adult.

People who want a show-quality Persian should buy one from a breeder.

People sometimes can adopt Persians from animal shelters.

Many Persian breeders live in the United States and Canada. People who want to find a local Persian breeder can attend cat shows. Cat shows are good places to talk to breeders and see their cats. People also should ask breeders for references. Other people who have bought cats from the breeders can act as references. These owners can describe their experiences with the breeders.

Pet Stores

People also can buy Persians at pet stores. Pet stores may have Persians for sale or may be able to get them from local breeders.

Many pet stores are clean and sell healthy animals. But people should check out a store before they buy a pet from it. Buyers should visit the store and ask store workers where they get their animals. Buyers should look closely at the animals to make sure the animals look healthy and alert. The animals' cages should be large, comfortable, and clean. The animals should have plenty of food, fresh water, and toys.

Animal Shelters

Many people adopt cats from animal shelters. These places keep unwanted animals and try to find homes for them.

An animal shelter can be a good place to adopt a cat for several reasons. People who adopt a pet from an animal shelter may save the pet's life. Many more animals are brought to shelters than there are people available to adopt them. Animals that are not adopted often are euthanized. Shelter workers euthanize animals by injecting them with substances that stop their breathing or heartbeat.

Animal shelters also can be a less expensive way to adopt a pet. Most shelters charge only a small fee. Some veterinarians provide discounts on medical services for shelter animals.

Shelters do have some disadvantages. Shelters often have mixed-breed pets available for adoption instead of purebred animals such as the Persian. People interested in adopting a Persian can contact a shelter. They can ask shelter workers to contact them when a Persian is brought to the shelter.

Another problem with shelter animals is that their histories often are unknown. Shelter workers usually do not know anything about the animals' parents, health, or behavior. Some owners may adopt cats with medical or behavioral problems. Shelter cats also seldom have papers showing that they are registered with official cat organizations. Owners who do not have registration papers for their cats cannot exhibit them in cat shows.

Rescue Organizations

People interested in adopting a purebred Persian may want to contact a breed rescue organization. These organizations are similar to shelters in

Some Persians adopted from breed rescue organizations may have registration papers.

some ways. Breed rescue organization members find unwanted or neglected animals. They care for the animals and try to find new owners to adopt them. People usually can adopt the animals for a small fee.

Breed rescue organizations are different from shelters in some ways. They usually rescue just one breed. They rarely euthanize animals. Most animals from breed rescue organizations are purebred. They even may be registered.

Chapter 5

Caring for a Persian

Persians are strong, healthy cats. With good care, Persians can live 15 or more years.

Indoor and Outdoor Cats

Some cat owners allow their cats to roam outdoors. This practice is not safe. Cats that roam outdoors have greater risks of developing diseases than cats that are kept indoors. Outdoor cats also face dangers from cars and other animals.

Owners of indoor cats need to provide their cats with a litter box. Owners fill the box with small bits of clay called litter. Cats eliminate waste in these litter boxes. Owners should clean the waste out of the box each day and change the litter often. Cats are clean animals. They may refuse to use a dirty litter box.

With good care, Persians can live 15 or more years.

Both indoor and outdoor cats need to scratch. Cats mark their territories by leaving their scent on objects they scratch. Cats also scratch to release tension and keep their claws sharp. This habit can be a problem if cats choose to scratch on furniture, carpet, or curtains. Owners should provide their cats with scratching posts. They can buy scratching posts at pet stores or make them from wood and carpet.

Feeding

Persians need a high-quality diet. Most pet foods available in supermarkets or pet stores provide a balanced, healthy diet.

Some cat owners feed dry food to their cats. This food often is less expensive than other types of food. Dry food can help keep cats' teeth clean. It will not spoil if it is left in a dish.

Other owners feed moist, canned food to their cats. This type of food should not be left out for more than an hour. It will spoil if it is left out for too long.

Some owners feed both types of food to their cats. This variety helps prevent the cat from becoming bored with its diet.

Persians need a high-quality diet of dry or moist cat food.

Cats need to drink fluids to stay healthy. Owners should make sure their cats' bowls always are filled with fresh, clean water. Most cats like the taste of milk. But milk can upset adult cats' stomachs.

Grooming

Persians' long, thick coats must be groomed with a wide-toothed metal comb every day. A

Persian's fur sometimes will clump together in a mat. Owners should not cut out the mats with scissors. Owners who do this may accidentally cut the Persian's skin. Cutting out mats also can damage the appearance of the cat's coat. Owners can use a small-toothed comb to comb out small mats in the fur.

Most cats do not need baths. But Persians' long coats should be bathed about once every three months. Owners should use a shampoo made for cats. Most cats resist getting wet. It is best to start bathing Persians when they are kittens. They then become used to being bathed.

Persians sometimes develop dark stains around their eyes. Persians' large eyes and flat faces allow tears to easily leak out of their eyes. The tears sometimes contain tiny organisms called bacteria. The bacteria will stain Persians' fur. Owners should clean around their Persians' eyes every day with a moistened tissue or cloth.

Some owners take their Persians to groomers. These workers are trained to bathe, comb, and brush cats and other animals. Owners should only take Persians to groomers

Persian cats sometimes develop dark stains around their eyes.

who have training and experience in working with longhaired cats.

Nail Care
The tip of a cat's claw is called the nail. Persians need their nails trimmed every few weeks. Trimming helps reduce damage if cats scratch on carpets or furniture. It also protects cats from infections caused by ingrown nails. Infections can occur when a cat does not sharpen its claws often.

Owners can give Persians medicines that prevent hairballs from lodging in the cat's digestive system.

The claws then grow into the pad or bottom of the paw.

It is best to begin trimming a cat's nails when it is a kitten. The kitten will become used to having its nails trimmed as it grows older. Veterinarians can show owners how to trim their cats' nails with a special nail clipper.

Dental Care

Persians also need regular dental care to protect their teeth and gums from plaque. This coating of bacteria and saliva causes tooth decay and gum disease. Dry cat food helps remove plaque from cats' teeth. Owners also should brush their cats' teeth at least once a week. They can use a special toothbrush made for cats or a soft cloth. They also should use a toothpaste made for cats. Owners should never use toothpaste made for people. Cats may become sick if they swallow it.

Brushing may not be enough to remove the plaque from older cats' teeth. They may need to have their teeth cleaned once each year by a veterinarian.

Health Problems

Persians can have some health problems. They often get hairballs. Cats often swallow fur as they groom their coats with their tongues. This fur can form into a ball in a cat's stomach. The cat then vomits the hairball. Large hairballs can become lodged in a cat's digestive system. A veterinarian then may have to perform an operation to remove these hairballs.

Regular combing is the best way to prevent hairballs. Combing removes loose fur before the cat can swallow it. Owners also can give Persians medicines that prevent hairballs. These medicines contain petroleum jelly. The jelly coats the hairballs in the cat's stomach. This helps the hairballs pass harmlessly in the cat's waste.

Persians' short noses can cause them to have breathing problems. These problems may lead to respiratory illnesses. Veterinarians treat these illnesses with medicines called antibiotics.

Some Persians can develop a serious illness called polycystic kidney disease. This disease usually occurs in older cats. It causes the cats' kidneys to stop working properly. Polycystic kidney disease often is fatal.

Polycystic kidney disease is an inherited disease. These diseases are passed down from the cat's parents. Good cat breeders test their cats for inherited diseases such as polycystic kidney disease. They do not breed animals that have serious diseases. Good breeders also tell owners if a cat's parents had any health problems.

Veterinarian Visits

Persians must visit a veterinarian regularly for checkups. Most veterinarians recommend yearly visits. Older cats may need to visit a veterinarian two or three times a year. More

Persians' short noses can cause them to have breathing problems that can lead to respiratory illnesses.

frequent checkups will help a veterinarian spot any health problems in older cats.

An owner who adopts a Persian should make a checkup appointment as soon as possible. The veterinarian will check the Persian's heart, breathing, internal organs, eyes, ears, mouth, and coat.

The veterinarian also will give vaccinations to the Persian. These shots of medicine help prevent serious diseases. These diseases include rabies,

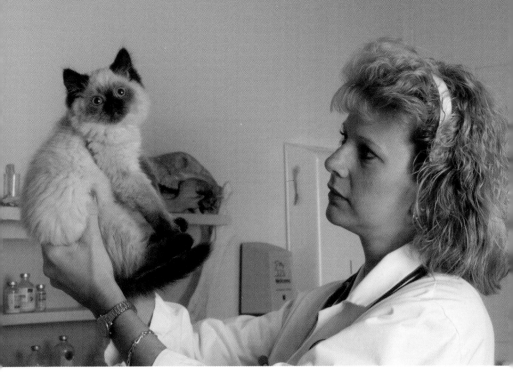

Regular visits to the veterinarian are an important part of cat ownership.

feline leukemia, and feline panleukopenia. Rabies is a deadly disease that is spread by animal bites. Most states and provinces have laws that require owners to vaccinate their cats against rabies. Feline leukemia attacks a cat's immune system. It leaves the cat unable to fight off infections and other illnesses. Feline panleukopenia also is known as feline distemper. This disease causes fever, vomiting, and death. Cats also can be vaccinated against several respiratory diseases that cause breathing or lung problems.

Cats should receive some vaccinations each year. They receive others less often. Breeders have information on which vaccinations Persians need. Cats that are kept indoors may not need all vaccinations. Owners should keep a record of their cats' vaccination dates. This record helps owners make sure that their cats have received all the vaccinations that they need.

Veterinarians also spay female cats and neuter male cats. These surgeries make it impossible for cats to breed. All cats should be spayed or neutered unless their owners want to breed them. The surgeries keep unwanted kittens from being born. They also help prevent diseases such as infections and cancers of the reproductive organs.

Spayed and neutered cats usually have calmer personalities than cats that are not spayed or neutered. They also are less likely to wander away from home to find mates.

Regular visits to the veterinarian are an important part of cat ownership. Owners and veterinarians can work together to help Persians live long, healthy lives.

Ears

Nose

Whiskers

Ruff

Paws

Tail

Coat

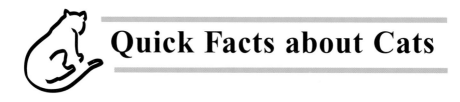

Quick Facts about Cats

A male cat is called a tom. A female cat is called a queen. A young cat is called a kitten. A family of kittens born at one time is called a litter.

Origin: Shorthaired cat breeds descended from a type of African wildcat called *Felis lybica*. Longhaired breeds may have descended from Asian wildcats. People domesticated or tamed these breeds as early as 1500 B.C.

Types: About 40 domestic cat breeds exist. The Cat Fanciers' Association recognizes 33 of these breeds. The smallest breeds weigh about 5 to 7 pounds (2.3 to 3.2 kilograms) when grown. The largest breeds can weigh more than 18 pounds (8.2 kilograms). Cat breeds may be either shorthaired or longhaired. Cats' coats can be a variety of colors. These colors include many shades of white, black, gray, brown, and red.

Reproduction: Most cats mature at 9 or 10 months. A sexually mature female cat goes into estrus several times each year. Estrus also is called "heat." During this time, she can mate with a male. Kittens are born about 65 days after breeding. An average litter includes four kittens.

Development: Kittens are born blind and deaf. Their eyes open about 10 days after birth. Their hearing develops at the same time. They can live on their own when they are 6 weeks old.

Life span: With good care, cats can live 15 or more years.

Sight: A cat's eyesight is adapted for hunting. Cats are good judges of distance. They see movement more easily than detail. Cats also have excellent night vision.

Hearing: Cats can hear sounds that are too high for humans to hear. A cat can turn its ears to focus on different sounds.

Smell: A cat has an excellent sense of smell. Cats use scents to establish their territories. Cats scratch or rub the sides of their faces against objects. These actions release a scent from glands between their toes or in their skin.

Taste: Cats cannot taste as many foods as people can. For example, cats are not very sensitive to sweet tastes.

Touch: Cats' whiskers are sensitive to touch. Cats use their whiskers to touch objects and sense changes in their surroundings.

Balance: Cats have an excellent sense of balance. They use their tails to help keep their balance. Cats can walk on narrow objects without falling. They usually can right themselves and land on their feet during falls from short distances.

Communication: Cats use many sounds to communicate with people and other animals. They may meow when hungry or hiss when afraid. Cats also purr. Scientists do not know exactly what causes cats to make this sound. Cats often purr when they are relaxed. But they also may purr when they are sick or in pain.

Words to Know

breeder (BREED-ur)—someone who breeds and raises cats or other animals

estrus (ESS-truss)—a physical state of a female cat during which she will mate with a male cat; estrus also is known as "heat."

euthanize (YOO-thuh-nize)—to painlessly put an animal to death by injecting it with a substance that stops its breathing or heartbeat

Himalayan (hi-muh-LAY-uhn)—a Persian cat with markings similar to those of a Siamese cat

neuter (NOO-tur)—to remove a male animal's testicles so that it cannot reproduce

spay (SPAY)—to remove a female animal's uterus and ovaries so that it cannot reproduce

vaccination (vak-suh-NAY-shun)—a shot of medicine that protects a person or animal from disease

veterinarian (vet-ur-uh-NER-ee-uhn)—a doctor who is trained to treat the illnesses and injuries of animals

To Learn More

Fogle, Bruce. *The Encyclopedia of the Cat.* New York: D K Publishing, 1997.

Kallen, Stuart A. *Persian Cats.* Checkerboard Animal Library. Edina, Minn.: Abdo & Daughters, 1996.

Quasha, Jennifer. *Persian Cats.* Kid's Cat Library. New York: PowerKids Press, 2000.

Seymour, Juliet. *Guide to Owning a Persian Cat.* Popular Cat Library. Philadelphia: Chelsea House Publishers, 1999.

Stone, Lynn M. *Persian Cats.* Read All about Cats. Vero Beach, Fla.: Rourke, 1999.

You can read articles about Persians in *Cat Fancy* and *Cats* magazines.

Useful Addresses

American Cat Association (ACA)
8101 Katherine Avenue
Panorama City, CA 91402

Canadian Cat Association (CCA)
220 Advance Boulevard
Suite 101
Brampton, ON L6T 4J5
Canada

Cat Fanciers' Association (CFA)
P.O. Box 1005
Manasquan, NJ 08736

The International Cat Association (TICA)
P.O. Box 2684
Harlingen, TX 78551

Persian and Himalayan Cat Rescue
305 Ross Drive
Mill Valley, CA 94941

Internet Sites

American Veterinary Medical Association Presents—Care for Pets
http://www.avma.org/care4pets

Canadian Cat Association (CCA)
http://www.cca-afc.com

Cat Fanciers' Association (CFA)
http://www.cfainc.org

Cat Fancy
http://www.animalnetwork.com/cats/default.asp

The International Cat Association (TICA)
http://www.tica.org

Persian and Himalayan Cat Rescue
http://www.persiancats.org

Index